Date: 5/28/20

811.6 CHA
Chabitnoy, Abigail,
How to dress a fish /

HOW TO DRESS A FISH

WESLEYAN POETRY SERIES

HOW

Abigail Chabitnoy

TO

DRESS

A

FISH

Wesleyan University Press | Middletown, Connecticut

Wesleyan University Press
Middletown CT 06459
www.wesleyan.edu/wespress
© 2019 Abigail Kerstetter
Manufactured in the United States of America
Designed by Mindy Basinger Hill
Typeset in Garamond Premier Pro

Library of Congress Cataloging-in-Publication Data
available upon request

Hardcover ISBN: 978-0-8195-7848-8
Paperback ISBN: 978-0-8195-7849-5
Ebook ISBN: 978-0-8195-7850-1

5   4   3   2   1

FOR MICHAEL, ADRIAN, AND NIKIFOR

CONTENTS

Family Ghosts   *1*

I

Fox Hunting   *5*
Family History   *7*
Family ~~Ghosts~~ History   *8*
[grocery list, July 26, 2015]   *9*
Shebutnoy   *12*
Distance of Articulation   *14*
[*Grandfather*, fig. 1]   *17*
[Boy, bear, bird?]   *18*
[(fish)]   *19*
[Observe the Indian as subject]   *21*
[(never so much fish)]   *22*
[The earth was hollow around my feet.]   *23*
Elocution Lessons   *24*
[(   )]   *28*
[*Grandfather,* fig. 2]   *29*
[fig. 3]   *30*
[fig.]   *31*
[(shark)]   *32*
[Not even bone.]   *33*
Lessons in Articulation   *34*
[*Grandfather*, fig. 5]   *35*
[Line. ~~November.~~ *post-fall month.*]   *36*
Dream with Shark   *39*
Survey of Resource Articulation   *40*
[It was winter]   *42*

II

[Only the beginning is true]   *45*
[. . . the bodies were too soft.]   *46*
Early She Works with Bodies   *47*
[(conditionally)]   *49*
[Pyrrha did not turn back]   *50*

She Gets Her Power from the Water   *51*

[every able body]   *53*

[In a box]   *54*

Ways to Sustain   *55*

[some burning persists]   *56*

[I turned fish]   *58*

Dream with Shark   *59*

[In a pile of available bodies]   *60*

[The dream is only trees]   *61*

[she fell down dead]   *62*

Let's begin again   *63*

[fig. with ghosts]   *65*

[(That's not how) the one from the water survived.]   *66*

Qawanguq with Fox   *67*

[No one expected a flood]   *68*

[. . . the smell of fish baking]   *69*

[The water rose.]   *70*

Qawanguq with House   *71*

III

History Lesson   *75*

Collection Object   *77*

Before There Was a Train   *91*

[She coughed and the women came out]   *92*

Family History   *94*

Family   story   *96*

   m y   story   *98*

         or   *100*

[not a fish]   *102*

[I was only a girl]   *103*

As Far as Records Go   *104*

Articulation of Distance; Or, The Hero Is Daily
   Called to Mind   *107*

In Communion with the Non-Breathing   *108*

[shallow bodies]   *109*

Family Ghosts   *110*

Ways to Sustain   *113*

Re-articulation   *115*

~~Manipulating Manifesting~~ (Re)Generating Landscapes   *116*

[Only the beginning is true]   *119*

ADDENDUM

How to Make a Memorial   *123*

Ways to Skin a Fish: A Genealogical Survey   *129*

Notes   *133*

Acknowledgments   *137*

FAMILY GHOSTS

Michael I wrote you
a story   I didn't know
what you did
what we did
if I should dig
you up   but
it didn't feel right
you should remain so far
from the sea
it didn't feel right
I couldn't see you

Is this the shape these things should take?

I

FOX HUNTING[i]

Last winter I [had a thought, go out],[ii]   hunt foxes.
[iii]

                                    , and, having come
to the opening of a little hut   , I entered it
and apparently there was a fox there,   I didn't
see , but when it was seen and pointed   to me
I could shoot

                              I ran

            , but running after it I
                  finally lost my breath

                                    under a rock,
                        pulled   from there
      ,   then I walked   and walked
                              , and   seemed to
be a fox   but   didn't see , but
      started to run again,   shot ,   so
I came back   two   .

      After   I   went to sleep,
      the   day   got up again

to hunt fox [.]   I passed

                                    to the other side
      one fox
                                          up the hill
                  thinking how   I was

                        a piece
            daylight   the hill

                                    the isthmus,
            the north side,
a storm   5

the sea,
the canyon

a fire   a little cave
the night
                    entered
        until the morning,
    the wind

            a pit in the snow
slept in   until the morning,   daylight

    descended

        from
            foxes
    and   steam
        and went home
.

---

[i] *Told by* ███████████, ████, *August, 1909. Cylinders 25 and 26 (four minutes and forty-five seconds). Transcribed and translated into Eastern Aleut by* ███████ *and* ████████ *with the help of* ███████████, *Umnak, 1910. Of the paired lines, the first is Attuan, the second Eastern Aleut. The written text differs in several spots from the cylinders. New York Public Library Manuscript 61.*

[ii] Contamination (or copying mistake).

[iii] Some words missing

FAMILY HISTORY

NAME: *Michael Chabitnoy*

1. Are you married and if so to whom? *Yes! To L▮▮▮ M. Z▮▮▮ of Lebanon, Pa.* [white]

2. What is your present address? *Hershey, Pa*

3. Where can I find you? Our aunt? Any relations?

4. What is your present occupation? *Moulding chocolate*

5. Tell [me] something of your present home. *I have a nice home and has all conveniency in it.*

6. What property in the way of land, stock, buildings, or money do you have? *None.*

7. What other positions have you held since leaving Carlisle? *None*

8. Why did you stay   in Pennsylvania?

9. Why didn't you stay   with our aunt?

10. Tell me anything else of interest connected with your life:

11. Tell me anything:

FAMILY ~~GHOSTS~~ HISTORY

DESCRIPTIVE AND HISTORICAL RECORD OF STUDENT

Degree of Indian Blood: Full

Well developed.

Normal.

Normal.

Normal.

Father. Dead. *Yes.* Traumatized.
Mother. Dead. *Yes.* Heart Trouble. (*bad heart.*)
Brother. Dead. *1.* Whooping Cough.
Sister. Dead. *1.* ?

(Aunt.)

Titiani.
  Unga,
    Alaska.

Living. *?* Condition of Health. *?*

There wasn't an aunt.

There wasn't an aunt
until five years later. *March 16, 1907.*

(At which point)

8

Michael Chabitnoy.
Tribe, *Alaskan.* Tribe, *Aleut.* Agency, *Baptist Orphanage, Wood Island.*
(otherwise listed *Michael Shepednoy.* Nation, *Alent.*)

was readmitted.

Michael Chepednoy. Nation, *Alent.*
returned to school without permission. *June 21, 1905.*

Conduct. *very good.*

April 10, 1909.
Student. *Michael Chabitnoy.* Nation, *Aleut.*
went on an outing and did not return.

JULY 26, 2015 [written around a grocery list]

[Side 1]

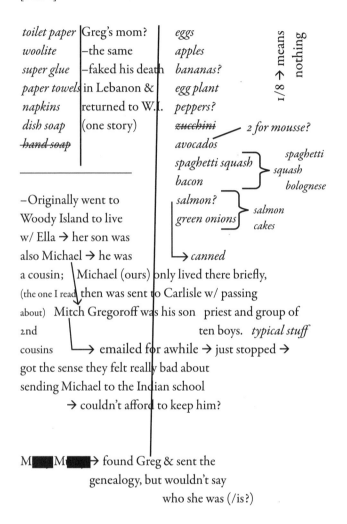

toilet paper | Greg's mom?
woolite | –the same
super glue | –faked his death
paper towels | in Lebanon &
napkins | returned to W.I.
dish soap | (one story)
~~hand soap~~

eggs
apples
bananas?
egg plant
peppers?
~~zucchini~~ — 2 for mousse?
avocados
spaghetti squash ⎫ spaghetti
bacon ⎬ squash
salmon? ⎫ bolognese
green onions ⎬ salmon
⎭ cakes
↳ canned

1/8 → means nothing

–Originally went to
Woody Island to live
w/ Ella → her son was
also Michael → he was
a cousin; ⟍ Michael (ours) only lived there briefly,
(the one I read then was sent to Carlisle w/ passing
about) Mitch Gregoroff was his son   priest and group of
2nd   ten boys. *typical stuff*
cousins ⟶ emailed for awhile → just stopped →
got the sense they felt really bad about
sending Michael to the Indian school
        → couldn't afford to keep him?

M███ M████ → found Greg & sent the
            genealogy, but wouldn't say
                who she was (/is?)

10

[Side 2]

- Dad?
  - Bill & Cass
  - remarried Ralph (Lil did)
    ↳lived alone
    in apartment after Ralph
    died
  - pinnacle & puzzles on Sunday nights
  - ask Dad → would always get together (Bill &
    Gordon) & get "blitzed"
  - no one really told stories about
    "the Indian"
  ↳pic on train w/ "Jim Thorpe" → face
    rubbed out
  - Nana Lil didn't talk about it →
    she was remarried
- Bill's gf, Cass, all discriminated against
- Only really a couple generations (for dating "Indians") *1 Little,   2 Little,*
- Greg doesn't really recognize a lot   *3 Little*
  —of discrimination ▆▆▆▆
  these days
            ↗still goes every summer to AK
- T▆▆▆ C▆▆▆▆ → mom on Woody Island
  w/ E▆ C▆▆▆▆   ↗wrote a book
                Alaska's Konyag Country
                ↳❧ about us
- Michael's parents killed in <u>boating accident?</u>

Cause of Death: *traumatized (?)*

SHEBUTNOY (trans. *Salmon-fisher*)
(Michael) Chabitnoy. Aleut.
1886–1920.

Because they were "of the water."
Because they were given Russian names.
He was born with hushed words.
Because his mother had a bad heart and his father was traumatized.
They took him from the sea.

Because he came to the school charitably, before.
Because there is only one photo, after.
They told the skeptics, *yes, it can be done.*

Because it could be done.
Because "Indian Marries White Girl."
Because he died of consumption.
There are words I can't say.

Because he was survived by two sons.
Because they were called half-breed.
Because that second son took to drink.
I've always been afraid of the sea.

Because it doesn't mean *salmon-fisher*.
Because I need to know I can say these words.
Because it means "mischievous, energetic."
Mischievous men (and women) fish for salmon energetically.

Because he was an orphan.
Because in summer, my skin turns redder than my father's.
Because they asked my mother, *Is she adopted?*

Because I too am of the water.
Because I hear these words.
I will split my bones and fit my skin to the sea.
I will shape my mouth to angle these words with the wind.

DISTANCE OF ARTICULATION

When letters are lost
I think of you, Michael, alone
on a train and dressed
as an ordinary parcel
an acceptable body   *15 years old, crossing the whole of America.*

> (My father too has always been drawn
> to trains.)

Did you make it to Carlisle
with all your words?
with your real voice?
                    with all your teeth?

Four thousand, six hundred
twenty-one miles today
if by land.   (not counting each wave between
                    Woods and the Fox Islands)
Three thousand thirty-four
if a Raven flies.

I'd like to believe you flew—
raptors, too, fish salmon.   *How do you think they got there? the fox,*

I'd like to believe you flew
and when your young boy wings tired over Pennsylvania
and there was no more salmon
they caught you and fed you and asked you
for your name

and brought you home
where there were others

and brought you home
to listen.

In appearance, Chabitnoy's claims of being a full blooded Indian are fully substantiated. He is red and well built and possesses a strikingly characteristic face,

like a fox.

Grandfather, great-grandfather,
with ears like that—

Did they f[h]ear you?

Boy, bear, bird? Shark? Fox? I can see something wild – Michael
– a body
         poised to run. The only natural thing – is defiant
forward or back? – under scrutiny. *What's behind your back? What
was in you(r) hands?* feathers, fur or teeth? – how soft the deer
mouth, low the ground wherein a grave meets the second born

how did we come here
Michael
where (do) we go?

Did your mouth grow soft with age Michael   could you still chew
the *kiimak* – the little bones   Can you hear them breaking down – *You can't*
spit a fish in the water and expect it still

to swim—

I am afraid to put my face under
water   afraid of filling these lungs
until the strain on my line
pulls me under

mouth open

What's behind you(r back)?

OBSERVE THE INDIAN AS SUBJECT.

Another described the legacy as a blank space. A space that unlike a slate can not be written. A moth-eaten hole.

Native scholars[i] call it a soul wound, but my book isn't clear if these are Native American men (and women) who have become scholars, or white men with pipes and elbow patches who study Natives from armchairs. I used to adore them, the stories they'd tell. Did you ever feel such wind again, or did it move right through you? Was your coat already full of holes before you took your first step east?

---

[i] a wound is a wound is a mouth is a wound

I was trying to remember how to make salmon cakes for my parents.
I was trying to find other ways to make salmon, because I didn't have the
right ingredients. I didn't have access to the foods listed
in my Unangax cookbook. I didn't know how to use the fish
in the traditional way—I didn't think you could
throw the salmon back in the water, the bones,
I didn't think they would swim again.

I'm thinking now it was a sign: the rest of the week I had bad dreams.

> I threw away the salmon
> spine   perfect line
> wide white eyes

>   scattered
> in my meal
>   returned

> Threw out meat
> threw out egg
> each pea-sized disturbance

> In all the cans of fish
> never so much   never
> so much—

> I threw them in the waste pan
> and spent the evening
> looking

> for other bones
> I might have
> missed

> for nights
> I dreamed of other bodies
> escaping
>   and bad omens.

The earth was hollow

                                           around my feet.

My feet were wading earth and
rotted branches. Limbs the size of human thigh
and twigs that could fit a small child
hand.

          But no trees for them to have fallen
and soon I was buried to my waist and some of the branches
were curved like a bow – like ribs –
and some knotted evenly into a perfect spine
and the salt on the air was soured.

                            I mean, the stench became so bad

I had to leave the bodies where they lay.

Grandfather is sitting in the kitchen with "all conveniency" in his cup.

Mother says these things skip a generation.

> Q: Is it because "Indian" marries "white girl" produces
>   "half-breed" shortly after "Indian" dies? Because
>   only half the blood can hide, only half the bones come clean?
> A: *Where are you going with these?*

Figures from the CDC are inexact. They've been imprecise in
their correlations, and

There are a number of ways one might choose
to articulate the shape

dependent on distance   between tongue
and   how   many   teeth

̄̄̄̄̄̄̄̄̄̄̄̄̄̄̄̄̄̄̄̄̄̄̄̄
WWWWWWWWWWWWWWWWWWWW

I'm beginning to suspect their threats are crossed.

Leading causes of death:[1] Heart disease *bad heart* cancer unintentional
injuries *frequently following* consumption of alcohol *followed by* diabetes
chronic liver disease *higher rate of binge drinking* chronic lower respiratory
disease stroke suicide *social(?)* pneumonia *impaired judgment* kidney disease
. . . *this is all just speculation of [a] course*

---

[1] National Vital Statistics System, ██████████.
Deaths, 15 leading causes of[,] death by race: United States, ██, Page ██.

What constitutes   a bad heart?
What constitutes   social consumption?
                   intent?
                   a threat?
                   Cause
                           of death: *traumatized.*

     Q: *Are you trying to relate to me?*

Statistics are a soft science.
INSERT BLOOD REQUIREMENTS HERE.
[Disregard.]

"Not only in architecture, dress, and food did administrators and settlers try to
maintain home standards but also in generating the statistical information that
was deemed necessary by the national government."

Considerable energy goes into constructing suitable records
that are in the end
                           inadequate.

"Given enough time, these things can be redressed."

            A: Yes, I am trying to relate to you—
               Which of my bones are yours?
               How about some extra ones for my back?

        (My spine is prone to fracture. A body has needs
                      to know its limits.)

I think I've got the color down, except for my white sexed parts, my
mother parts. These are unresponsive.
                   White is a nervous shade,
              don't you think?
So easy to spoil.
I've been wearing white since the wedding. There are some stains,
as one might expect.
     Red and yellow, black and white . . .

I am precious on my mother's side.

"It is our generation's turn. That is, it's my turn, but
I don't feel the need. That is, I don't feel any real threat."

Observations: Although health outcomes among AIs are improving, large
disparities with other racial and ethnic groups in the United States remain.
Many health-related problems are directly linked to high rates of substance
use and abuse.

One mustn't rush to find a cause until we know

                                        all the facts are known.

It's just—
the bones these ▇▇▇ scientists keep digging up
remember where the blood escaped
                        there was blood in them
                        we buried—

I have inherited more skeletons than I can count. Such a weary weight
to conquer this mass.

Q: Statistically speaking,
                    Must I be old?
                    Must I be traditional?
                    Must I be fair?

Fair skinned, fair haired, neatly squared[2]?

---

[2] That means, "the right box on a demographic form"

A: The question of blood lies out the body.
    bodies

Guangkuta "Sugpianek" ap'rtaakiikut cuumi, nutaan ap'rtaaraakut Alutiit.

Can you put my *apaq* on the line? That is, my great- (in regarding distance)
apaq on this line? It is important that I reach him, that I follow the right
channels, a body
water will wash   away

                                        return me transparent to the sea.

> On weekends I can be found in museums trying to find the right
> face to wear in light of recovered records and evolving vocabulary.
> I am thinking a shark but a shark like any other predator
> looks as much man as monster the way
> these bodies are
> figured.

Results: Grandfather is crying, great-grandfather is crying. *Where are they
going, the children, and when // will they come back?*

            It means we-are-people.

Still, there's a chance, mother says:
these things skip a generation.

What if we were the fish?

"In appearance, Chabitnoy's claims of being a full blooded ~~Indian~~ are fully substantiated."

Today I learned I'm biracial. or mixed racial. ambiguously ethnic. I read it in a book, but I don't feel comfortable with any of these. Genocide elementary by comparison. Anybody can be outraged at a wrongful death. But wrongful living? I was comforted by the half white, half Mexican boy glowing beside me. Everyone wants to see ghosts, in theory.

That is to say, I still don't know how to fit this skin. I, too, am tall and well built
and in summer possess a strikingly characteristic face. And if I only run
a short distance, you can hardly tell the trouble with my back,
the fragmented bone attached by gristle, or not, or
floating just below the skin—

Did you make yourself wind to make up your size? – *How else is a fish*
accustomed to keeping its feet on the ground? – Why did you come
back? Did you forget which way the wind blowed?

One summer evening Mike Chabitnoy
and some boys killed a shark
off Wood Island Coast
and dragged the beast ashore.

(the other Mike,
the son,
the one who stayed
with our aunt)

One of them jumped on the thickest part
and out flew a large salmon
from its open mouth.

Another and another until
five large perfect fish leaped forth
amid screams from the children.

Were you
a shark
or something smaller?

They named the shark Jonah.

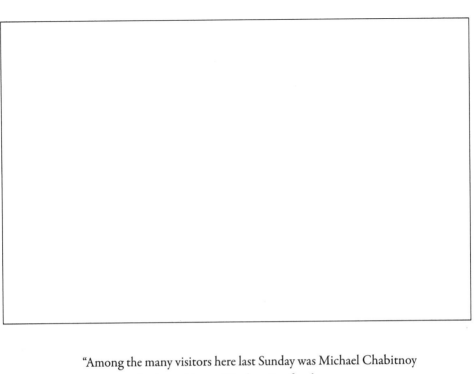

"Among the many visitors here last Sunday was Michael Chabitnoy
who is working at Hershey, Pa., for the summer.
'Mike' is also trying out for the Hershey baseball team."

Conduct : *good*

Why did you leave and then come back? Did you play with Jim Thorpe
in school 'Mike'? Did you eat pork and milk and green beans and butter?
Did you live in the Athletes' Quarters? Which tale are we in again Michael?
Who gets to be of-the-water? *Who gets to be people? above or below the sea –*

Isn't a shark just a fish after all?

It was winter. I was sweating. You and I were in a boat, going back to Unalaska and my body went cold to spite my discomfort. You can be wind. You can be feathers. You can be fur or fin and teeth. I am not even earth. Not even bone. But permafrost in a warming state. Cold, not cold enough. Porous. Full of holes. Not filled but

disappearing.

LESSONS IN ARTICULATION

He didn't tell us when he learned what it meant,
that they took their words from them.

If he were not an accountant, my father,
he might have been a historian. A fisherman. Or
he might have been nobody. He might have been unsettled.

Father, did you have these questions, when you were young with only
     your cousin, your aunt?
Father, did your father know?
Did your father tell you,

                         how he and his brother were called half-breed,
                              how he didn't know his father?
Did you read to your mother?
Did you read to your dog, until you could pronounce the words properly?
Did you eat Hershey's Chocolate toast sandwiches with your father?
Did your father read aloud from his bible, or
     did he keep his words from you?

               Father, did you dream then of salt sweeping your lungs, of sand
                              and volcanic rock beneath
                                   your feet, or snow?
                    Did you watch the birds as a boy for Company?
                         Did you try to give them names?

Father, did you play Indians?
     Or were you cowboys?
How did you feel, the way your father asked your mother
for a sandwich and a beer,

                    and a beer,

                                        like a man?
Mother says these things skip a generation.

I don't remember learning these words—

deprivation, decimation, assimilation,

relocation.

I don't remember Carlisle in my school books. Was it something
you showed me, Father, that summer
we toured all the battlefields?

If he were not an accountant, my father,
he might have been a historian.
But there was no value in these things,
no way he could convey.

I don't know when I learned what it meant,
they took our words from us.

In appearance, Chabitnoy's claims of being a full blooded
Indian are fully substantiated. ___ is long and well built
and possesses a striking face.

We know this one thing –

Grandfather, great-grandfather,
how many teeth do you have?

Sharks keep swimming

[Line. ~~November~~. *post-fall month*.]

Forgive me grandfather, great-grandfather, but I ~~can't help~~ think you remind me of a waiter in those pants. How does a factory worker get to be so white? That overcoat doesn't suit you Apaq. The body drowns, forgets to swim. *Goes soft*. I am trying to be beautiful in the current understanding, that is, I am trying to be current where drowning is beautiful. I am trying to be beautiful while drowning because I don't know how to swim – I don't know how to be a fish that is ~~I am~~—

In the sun I turn brown and almost
scaly. When I turn brown my cheekbones almost
look high enough for people
to ask me what I am

but my eyes are the wrong kind of brown and more
sea weed than sea and my face
is too long
and my bones
are too long

except for my spine—
        the kind of bones that get carried away
or down't.

And my hair is too fine
and requires too much
washing—

but when I smile
when no one's watching
I look almost
like a shark—

        white teeth surrounded by too much
pink.

DREAM WITH SHARK

I dreamt my mother placed me in the sun
to bake
      by the water

I bake so red
so hard

I couldn't take this new skin off

I couldn't cover this new skin with fur
or feathers
        not even hair

No other shape would adhere
to my new body
          only teeth—

no other shape could press into
my body

Mother, what do I do with these arms?
They won't bend Mother

    how do I move these arms?

SURVEY OF RESOURCE ARTICULATION

from TITLE 43 U. S. CODE CHAPTER 33

§ 1630. Claims Arising from Acquisition of Entitlement on behalf of Relocated
   Persons Resulting from Unintended Contamination of Transferred Qualities

Such persons begin to question—

(a) how the land will be used, for whom;   *(, the water—)*

(b) how one will use one's arms, for whom;

(c) how one is to understand these and other such provisions without knowing
the story; without hearing the story the way it is told; without hearing it
spoken; speaking:

> (a) I dream of the sea [*break*]
> since a girl.
>   [*pause*]
> Each time I die,
> I lay my body on a bed of shells [*broken*]
> hollowed to be strung. [*breathless*]
>   [*pause*]
> Each body having died [*break*]
> multiple, [*skip beat*] like misplaced boulders [*break*]
> erratic
>   [*wait*]
> like fire-rock [*breaking*],
> shape the shoreline.

(d) to what extent they are visible in their bodies;[b]

(e) whether stasis is a matter of upbringing;[c]

"It is cold
& wet &
the wind
lifts beads
of sweat
from the sea
& shrouds
the islands
in a soft
filtered
light."

[c] One can walk for days and still see major landmarks seemingly unchanged: the mountain remains a mountain any way you look at it.[d]

(f) where one should migrate when there is only one season;

(g) how it is here, in the beginning of the world, a mountain is a thing that grows;

(h) how it is, not here, removed, relocated, qualities are transferred, one acquires the persistence of mountains;

(i) how to be like the sea—

the line, the wave, shore.

---

[b] You can see the displaced when the ground amasses too much water, the weather becomes variable by degrees, breaking up through the permafrost in unexpected shades. All hell breaks loose as the tundra thaws. One begins to question, where are my relatives?   *(kinkut ilaten?)*

[d] How it is one can walk for days and still not see major landscapes

It was winter and I was sweating
The heat uncomfortable expecting snow
I get cold so easy my body forgets
I thought of you yesterday again in the wind
Going nowhere beside my self
What was the wind on Wood Island like?
Could you walk the other way
Umnak or Unalaska bound
Did it ever blow you right
Where [did] the world begin(s)

Tell me Michael where the world ends –
did you ever feel such wind again?

April 10, 1909.
Student. *Michael Chabitnoy.*
went on an outing and did not return.

II

Only the beginning is true
each time.

There was fire.

There was a flood.

There was one
                    she came from the water
who had to reshape the earth.

She had to throw her mother bones over her shoulders

                    each time

She had to throw her own bones
                            black fire-rock
                    bones
over her shoulders

and each rock she threw over her shoulders grew
                    from the belly

and life grew in them.

        iganagii

In the beginning the bodies were too soft.

They couldn't stand
upright.

They couldn't stand
by the water

      They folded in the wind
            in the beginning

So she made the bodies hard.
         she made the bodies too hard

The bodies were too hard and too many
to move—

      They had metal arms
      and metal hearts
            pulled from the sea

They were hungry.

Their bodies were hunger but   they couldn't move—
                    couldn't see
                    couldn't hear—
they perceived only rocks
and repurposed metal
          clack-clack-clack
fire

and salt
water
     to carry arms

They didn't know how to feed their hunger.

EARLY SHE WORKS WITH BODIES

She found the body by the water
    little bird
        where the water should not have been

Little bird must have fallen
    little bird
        could not swim

Perhaps little bird was struck
    by car or bigger bird—
        some days the road led straight into the sea

The salt and the sand rolled the body raw until its insides showed
    the breast exposed
        little bones

A BB grew in the womb

She shaped the sand around the bird
    little bird
she closed the wound over the BB

and started sticking feathers in the sand
    in little bird's heart
        where she thought they should be

Her mother came to take her home,
    grabbed her by the wrist and pulled

Don't play with dead things—
    dirty,
she said

But mama she's pregnant
     there's an egg
in here   [points to her belly]

a condition

always
                    each time

must not look back
                    each time
        she looked back

Pyrrha did not turn back
      when she was placed on Mount Parnassus.

Pyrrha did not look at her mother-children

The fire-headed one did not remain
on the mount.

The fire-headed one descended
      with the waters

She descended to the shores

and built her home
      where the winds began

She built her home out of the bones
washed by the flood

She sat under the ribs
of a great fish

      where she thought the belly ought to be

and she waited for the beginning
to be true

—————

She took a name
for beginning

She-gets-her-power-from-the-water

SHE GETS HER POWER FROM THE WATER

She removed her ribs and
buried them
in a row
        , having dreamt she would lose them

She slept and dreamed
       in her dreams
         she couldn't breathe

She couldn't breathe
in her dreams
there was no air

———

She woke to find her chest
was sand

her ribs were
rock

     her lungs fire
weeding
through the
        faults

Her body sand
was baking

She was baking in the sun
her body
      was

        in her belly
hard

    there was fire

———

She became hard

so she crawled to the sea and dipped her glass hands
in the water

In the water her hands became soft
and pliant

She dipped her body in the water

she pulled the water through her heart
through her lungs
into her belly

———

In the water she could move
freely
but above the water
she was hard and hot and could not
move

above the water
She was a red mouth   a wound
spitting fire

must be reshaped –
the body
depends

I went down to the water
to swim

I was afraid—

The water was black
and heavy to move through

It coated my skin
my summer-black skin

> *What a lovely body,*
> *is she adopted?*

They closed the beach
and filled bags with sand

with every able body

In a box they put me
                    spruce and pining
sealed with mud
hot and wetted with fire
                    with blood   under fire
                    and water
from the sea
                    until salt—

A woman upstairs dying
said
       our lives depend on your fullness
on your thought—

This woman   she took out her rib
and placed it in my chest

My mother then gave me her lung

Then other women did the same
until
I didn't fit

WAYS TO SUSTAIN

if this is not the way
these bones should be
if this is not the proper way
they should lie
clean with care
again
clean
each joint
    thorough
each wave
over   again
set aside enough skin
bleach in the sun
grow taut
    transparent
enough to reveal any shape
enough to remain water
tight
for crossing over

I woke on the face
water
        cool

but some burning persists—

I feel him now
in me
        is me
swelling

At the source
        at the water
I went to greet the sun

I went to the morning
        to fit its light in my mouth
to insist on being
                one
        -of-the-water

But inside I was fire
fire won't stamp out

The homes that stood around me
were exposed
        gray
                poured rock   and
    windpocked

The rooms all smoke   -
filled cavities
        wherein lungs and heart—

———

They put a songbird in the box with my body
      the women

something to eat
when I woke

      I thought he might have gone, my song

bird never sang—

I don't know
what the water wants

I filled my pockets with rocks
so when I would walk out on the water
my body would retain weight

on the solid sea
            beneath

The water filled me with sound
            until
I couldn't speak
            until
I turned fish
                        carried away
            in the current

not knowing
            what kind, monster

Why should I be the only one
in this place?

DREAM WITH SHARK

I was dreaming in the sea—

I decided my family
    should be there
in the sea I decided
    we all should be   there

I reached my arms into the water
    to my shoulders
and tried to hold the place
    in the sea we should be

When I felt a solid mass
    fill my arms I pulled

I pulled the head of a shark
    out of the water

―――――

        I pulled the head
out of the shark.

In a pile of available bodies
I was looking for the one with teeth

I was looking for one with enough teeth

Knocking the jaws out of line
            climbed into the maw
and I waited
                        behind the crowding rows

The dying thing outside sounded like a child

        a small body afraid

I closed my newly many mouth
and slipped back in-the-water

                        careful to keep swimming

I rocked my smaller self to sleep
inside the beast

Must be reshaped   the body
depends on your lungs
                        the women said

        How long can you hold your
tongue?

The dream is only trees   soft
flesh underfoot
          soft the fleshy moss that comes off the trees
in my hands
                    and pink
on an island without—

Her body became soft

She could feel a hardness sinking
down her clay chest

where she had no more ribs

    she reached inside

The hardness   now was in her stomach

    where her stomach ought to be

    were leafy greens
and a rock

The hardness   now had settled

in the leafy greens
    it had settled
    in her stomach

She pulled out the rock
it was warm
and wet
    and porous

and turned red against the salt air

It was warm and wet
when she pulled out the rock

when she pulled out the rock

    she fell down dead

Let's begin again

She fell down
She fell down

The body begins
she begins

After she fell down she laid for some time where it was dark
waiting for a body

> The women came
> in carrion skins

> In white carrion feathers the women came and ate the sickness

> They ate her liver
> and they ate her lungs
> and they ate her heart

> Red spilled down their throats

The girl out of the water could not see
without her eyes

> They took her girl eyes

> > Were they raven, crow
> > or raptor?

I'm looking for a more suitable heart
she said
> before they ate her tongue

You must speak without it
they said

Then they wrapped her bones
and left a body in the rock
                    in the mouth
for when the water
returned

        ixtalix

Find a place you feel comfortable and do it.
Purse your lips together   teeth parted   tongue
holding the weight of the roof
your mouth. Inhale

                              release.

Find a place you feel comfortable with ghosts.

Rumor has it you might wake spirits
this way   this talking
how the dead talk   not in word

                              but sound.

That's not how the one from the water
survived.

How could she survive
in a box?   in pieces?

Good Friday the waters came.

On the roof she found a woman
dying with potted plants
rotting in the over-salted air.

A hole opened up in the sky if she could just reach
this sky she could reach
the ground she needed

But she needed that neck to get through.
She needed that woman's neck.

She needed a medium
of authority
of consumption or
birthing or
a way to breathe otherwise.

She needed a neck
with a mouth.

QAWANGUQ WITH FOX

I was walking up some stairs in a building

Inside parts of the building were new
but no one lived there anymore

I passed a lucky fox head on the stairs—

> *But fox, where are your ears and your eyes and your tongue?*
> *where is your body, your bushy tail?*

The head slunk past without stopping

> *If a fox crosses your path, an opportunity will be given you*

so I followed it through the building to the roof
where the sky
                    and a woman lay dying

"I used to have a garden," she said

> *If a fox stops and looks at you, your ambitions will be fulfilled*

She took out her eyes and her tongue
and placed these in my hand

She took a fox tail from under her skirts
and fastened it to my spine
                              where it had forked
                    she joined the pieces

She ran her fingers over my ears
and they tickled like fur

When I looked up she didn't have any ears
any eyes
          any tongue
                    any tail

The head sat there
vacant in my direction

I put the fox eyes to my eyes
and I could see across the sea

I put the tongue in my pocket
      and picked my way down the stairs unseen
following the smell of tide

No one expected a flood
despite sea displacing
sea despite old waters
waking

While the waters walked
                        they talked

they kept their eyes on fire
but fire stayed put

They grew accustomed to the smoke
even liked the new sky—

    the way it coated their skin and mixed with beads of sweat

    the way it hid the whites of their eyes

    the way it settled on their tongues
the few remaining soft parts
down their throats

until they felt thick
and heavy

and full
                    with their own soot

We knew there would be trouble
when we saw smoke

    they told us to be still
  so we ran

The wild things knew
    before us

Not a bird remained

only a wall of hostile air
and the sea

    the smell of fish
baking

The water rose.

The burning one came on shore.

The space between cities
                    was reduced.

There are   causalities
        always

casualties, consolation prize.

QAWANGUQ WITH HOUSE

There was a house I needed
to go

I needed a home
    to survive
        to wait the fire
the flood where there were others
           with other
bodies

There was earth in them
        I dug
speaking
the dead with words

I dug my way back
      to survive the flood
into the earth

I had to know what I didn't know
    I didn't know
what kind of monster was I

You can't throw the fish
back in the water
and expect to swim—

So I dug.

I dug out a rib
and another's rib
    another

I dug deeper
    until

I reached the bottom of this

house I reached the cellar
where the center was cold

where I could hide

My body full of bodies.

III

HISTORY LESSON

Umnak, Unimak, Unalaska, Krenitzin
islands *largely mythological*

The violence increased in direct proportion to the
escalation of fur . . . [when] Big-Money entered the
. . . waters . . . [he] must have grown enormously.
since they were a warrior society War erupted in 1763
. . . ~~It is believed that~~ The conflict was triggered by
birching a small Aleut ~~hostage~~ boy who happened
to be a son of an important Aleut chief. This seems
unlikely in view of the fact that *invaders customarily
received short shrift* [the irritants do not] mention
such an occurrence.

All, however, stress that the hostility was general
and organized *in the Aleut manner.* Umnak
Aleuts claimed the honor *by ruse and surprise* for
themselves.

we know little of the situation Waging a campaign of
destruction . . . [i]n several encounters, with minimal
casualties to his own force, ~~Solov'iev~~ Solovey
~~reported about~~ killed 200 warriors, a tremendous
loss in ~~able-bodied men~~ Real People ~~killed~~. *(we know
little of the situation, which was largely mythological)*

[The Destroyer] then proceeded to destroy *without
ruse or surprise* any *baidarkas* found on premises, and
to break throwing boards, darts, spears *culture* and
bows and arrows. *by these means* [The Destroyer]
destroyed ~~not~~ people ~~so much~~ as [his] means of
survival. It is by these means, and not by genocide,
which is largely mythological *(we know little)* that
he broke . . . and entered Aleut folklore.

largely mythological This man, who in 1970 would be remembered by Aleut chiefs of Unalaska as the Destroyer, understood and respected the Aleuts.

[NOTE TO SELF: After this poem, include definitions of GENOCIDE.]

COLLECTION OBJECT

GIINARUAQ
Currently on view

When I decided to be Indian
                they were everywhere.
There are a lot of Indians
    in the lower forty-eight.

I am learning by my hand
             how big my hand is—

How many homes on this street
                     are still haunted?
We were taken to learn
             how to cut trees
to live here
          how to make clothes
to hide our selves
            how to bend steel
and other metal
          with enough pressure
and fire
      how to yield
to desired shapes
        how at first
we didn't know
         how to fire our arms
to fit our bodies
       to metal,

At first we didn't know
             how to leave here
to survive—
      didn't know how
to dig
    the bodies, how

to recover
        the faces, the labrets
the weight that was fastened to bone

                once the barracks were reoccupied

once the children were sent home.
        How.
I am asking.

———

We didn't need to teach them how
to draw fish.

They didn't need to teach us how
to sew the skin.

(Don't ask me to identify them—I haven't decided which yet,
or whom.)

        I never learned to sew
        or gut a fish.

        I didn't understand how to use the objects
        archaeologists uncovered—

        Where is my shovel?

          Iksak ipegtuq
          Siilaq ipegtuq
          Mingqun kakiwigmi et'uq

        I am putting bait on my hook

                —or the records
                recovered from the archives.

> Michael Chabitnoy, an Alaskan exstudent,
> is one of the many Carlislers who is making
> good out in the world. He has been in the
> employment of the Hershey Candy Co.,
> for about two years and is now earning
> from four to five and a half dollars a day.

A woman told me I was a witch, a [Navajo word for witch,
or something approximate]
    (I was wearing my thumb on the wrong ring, or
        I was wearing my Hopi ring on the wrong thumb,
    the stone having fallen out of the Peruvian ring I otherwise wore;
        I hadn't decided if it was real)—

but I am not Hopi or Navajo
               so it was ok,
        I guess.
                    (Do they call them Indians, in Peru?)

She asked me, this woman, why have you come here, she asked me
        "are you trying to relate to me   something?"

Before we were Russian.
They told us
        we were Russian.
It means *salmon-fisher* in Russian.
                      Doesn't it?

One face is not enough
                              to adapt
to survive
                              to be both predator and prey
and a shark is after all
                              not so different:
blood, and other body—
                              after all, a little wood and paint and a century
                              in the earth
and a man's face might assume
                              a shark in an appropriate style.

———

After ending the week in the margins of creative industry
          (editing others' errors with as little voice
                    as I could muster)
I took a field trip to Denver with the other women.

We ate Indian tacos and fry bread
in an Indian restaurant
                    and   I thought
                              I am here,   with these women
                              I am.

Together we admired the T-shirts on the wall with their slogans—

                              No reservations needed.

———

It didn't look like a shark. It didn't look like it was buried
for a hundred years.
                              Must it be old
in order to be,   to be authentic?
in order to be an authentic Amerindian artifact?
          (That word has gone out of fashion—nowadays
                    it is a "heritage object"—)

It still doesn't look like the shark   I was expecting
        and it takes me awhile   to find it in the sea
            of faces mounted on the wall.

————

When I was a girl my parents took us to the Four Corners
        to go site-seeing.

"Do you like Native American things? Then you must go
to the Southwest."
        (I was wearing my raven pendant, the one from the wrong
            village I bought at another museum, and a cheap circle
        charm with "tribal" etchings I had bought for six dollars at a
            rock shop in Old Town; it said I would come to no harm in
            water, and I took it for a sign.
        I wore a dream catcher in my right ear and a feather in my left.)

————

                    It does no good to tell these people you were there.
                                It matters to them
                                that they can help you—
like the woman at another museum, from Alaska, the one
        from Connecticut who had moved there and collected "heritage
        objects" indiscriminately—

        "Have you been?"
        "Yes, I—"
        "Oh, you must go!"

————

I went to Denver with the women because I needed new material.
                    I needed a second hand.

Naama lapaat'kaaqa?

The fishhook is sharp
The awl is sharp
The needle is in the sewing bag

I'm putting bait on my hook

———

"For a time, we were strictly rock people," the Pueblo girl said
between bounces in the back seat of the passenger van. Out the window,

"All the houses on this street are haunted."

———

"What a shame," my mother said
                     "that they've become encumbered by television,
all these wires are spoiling
               the panorama.
What a shame
               they are not living like Indians   anymore—
poor Indians."

———

In my memories, often my mother   becomes a scapegoat.

A Daughter must be faultless
in her presentation.

       "Guard your tongue in youth," said the old chief, "and in age
       you may mature a thought that will be of service to your people."

(I read this in a book someone gave me, *The Wisdom of the NATIVE*
AMERICANS.)

———

My father bought us each a kachina doll so they would be less poor
        so we would have something to remember them by.
                We bought souvenirs from all the reservations.
                    The careful beading on my medallion
                        snapped before we'd made it home.

        (Later on that same trip, in Albuquerque, I watched men play their
        flute music like it was magic while my parents wandered in and out of
        shops. I looked down into the square at their performance. The man was
        singing,
                he stared up at me on the balcony and I stared back intently.
                I was too young to know there was something not quite right
                in that stare.)

        ———

It's a bear—on my witch ring. You've heard (of course)
        of the great Kodiak bear, and
        Wood Island

                                        is just across a narrow channel

we are from

                                        according to the records.

(Of course, this connection has
been retrofitted: a deliberate hole in a fine sheet
of metal laid over a solid band   fired to fit.)

        ———

        I guess we are Aleut after all.

*They told us
we were Russian.*

        ———

I wouldn't have even known there was a shark
        if it wasn't for the placard on the wall.

But labels, too, can be misleading.

A vague field of grave-shaped holes
smooth under fresh white
paint:

Here lies

———

            A girl,
when I was, I was careless
            with my dolls   I pulled out their feathers   I popped
their wooden arms off   Now they lay prostrate
                     on their backs   sick men in cubbies where
I show them

But I still don't know the names
                     and it only takes one small cloud
in an otherwise blue sky
                     across the sun to make me shiver
to raise the hairs on my arms
                     and I wonder,
would I be able to survive
                     in the islands North, I wonder,
would I be able to keep my body
                     warm there
where lay my family bones?

———

I saw a bear in Pennsylvania once.

No one believed me.

Use the mask, giinaruaq (*"like a face"*):

———

When we were through with the exhibits we wandered through
        the gift shop. I was hoping to find a recreation
of Warhol's commodified Indian to hang
                on my wall.

There was only the usual jewelry
                        and some baskets,
woven horsehair—
                        someone knew the woman who made them;
the cost
        staggering in ways only a history of genocide, of
subjection, willed extinction, of defiance
                                can justify.

We would not pay so much for ordinary goods.

Are these earrings authentic?
                        Are they Native American   made?
Were they sustainably harvested?

———

It matters where we break the line.

———

                        I am painting my mask. Like travelers
                                the faces
                                        were painted red.

———

I heard we were not Indians after all.
I heard we were our own not-Indian-*indigenous* people.

It's complicated.

We call them *naked ones.*

(*They:*)
Matarngasqat Camani amlertut.

———

Mix the pigments with oil or blood
to bind.

Naked, we are unafraid   un-
encumbered.

Encumbered, present arms to strike
         paint ourselves
              targets
              —

              Strike here,   and
                        here.

Strike here where I have let my color show,
         where I have painted myself fatal

                   with blood.

KRaasiyaqa maaskaaqa

———

I made a pair of earrings. Ivory and turquoise
plastic.

They cannot be found for sale anywhere else in the world.

I imagine the earrings I bought at the Heritage Center in Anchorage
         were made the same—
                   a nail, some beads, a pair of pliers and
              the right amount of history, of blood.
                        (Truthfully, I was disappointed when I learned
                        it was so simple.)

When will I be old?

———

There are a lot of naked ones in the lower forty-eight. At a glance
they could be people under so much skin.

Or birds,
25 birds for 25 girls, for 1,200, for 4,000—

———

A girl a father and a star
don't have to look how they're supposed to.
And after all, we were
(*we are*)
water people.
Why not be sharks?

Or a bear, like those stars,

or a short-eared owl—something
that burrows despite itself,   something

that excavates.

"There is a storm about
our ears":

If you turn those stars upside down they resemble nothing so

much   as

a   shovel,

oil or blood—

———

One face is not enough
                    surface   to bear enough
                                              weight—how many would it take
to stop a bullet?

———

26 September 1745. Targets for practice were found in abundance.

Thank the merchant from Okhotsk, Grigor Shelikof, the benevolent,
    the founder of Alaska.

Under other management advances were made in science:
                              1764. One Capt. Solovief was reported to
                              experiment, among other things, upon the
                              penetrative power of his bullets by binding 12
                              Aleuts in a row.

Welcome, *How?* New World.
                                              You mix the blood with oil.

———

Nine.

———

The placard on the wall calls
                              the tall wooden man
Welcome Figure. 1900.
                    Chief Johny Scow.
Welcome being a matter of
                    perspective
requiring copper
          and arms.

I am teeth
          and shell
and skin—
          the shark doesn't look so different.

How old must I be?

———

These marks are not significant on land where we have lain.
       I heard through grave pines,
it doesn't take a sky of stars to suggest an arrow
          (though I suppose a spear would be more appropriate,
                    or a harpoon) . . .
It depends which way you look,
       how much fits at hand.
                    . . . a shovel . . .

———

I think the masks on my wall are all wrong
       from Hawaii, Africa, Costa Rica,   from everywhere
but home—
    I looked at the mask the placard told me would look like a shark
but all I saw was the green face of a man,
               looking dead

and not very old.

                    In the summer my skin tends red
               but the sun lightens my hair and my eyes
                      are already green,

                         not brown,

and old,   getting old.

———

I hide my inheritance behind my back
               swinging pendulum

my inverse infant—

              my body

is too conflicted

             from affront

to fit in my hand—

            The time is at hand for motives.

Motives must be held
accounted:

        I am looking for the body
           hanging
        round my neck
          pulling
            me
          for ward
        to the place I
      can see honestly, say,   I am not an Indian
                              not *not* an Indian—

———

I can say, *here,*
     and present not arms, but hands
outstretched for a mother
        my mother

       to any other,

 I can say,

       I am of the water,

I can say that
     I am.

BEFORE THERE WAS A TRAIN

I built my home
from perfumed skins
and crooked bones

       far from the rotting boat
They took
          the wrong shape

Sod   not ice   not body

not Other

Nikiiq

    Engluq nikiimek patumauq

The wrong tongue

By the time you read this
I will have forgotten how to say
    the house is covered with sod

            or home

Part of me wishes it had sunk
        it sank
          it is sinking

but these sentences have not been written

Only, *allrani suu'ut caqainek pukugtaartut*

               sometimes people salvage some stuff

She coughed and the women came out
      violently
She opened her mouth and coughed out
      a small bird
She coughed out matted fur
          and fish with faces
          and the rocks
          she had tried to eat
    until
there was nothing left inside her
                but water   and red

She coughed out the water
and the sea rushed to fill
the thirsting places

She took back fire
          black fire-rock
and wrapped her many-body
in mountain
        still and moving
        many and
             one

She wrapped her body in mountain
and dug her feet beneath the water
            she spilled
where soft
      she could feel a hardness moving
          outward

She could feel many hearts
                    hard hearts
each small disturbance
                         press
the small rooms of her chest

Each sound in her chest
a heart
        a rock
dislodging   soft in the water

        until

            She was no body

FAMILY HISTORY

Only the beginning is true.

There was an island
and an orphanage
and a boy.

There was a train and a country
to cross.

There was just a boy.
They took his words from him.

There was just a boy
and they took from him his words

                    so he could not speak with others
                    so he could not know there were others
                    so he was just a boy

We know there was a boy

alone.

Can I say these things if I am not that boy?

I don't know that boy

—that is—

I never spoke to that boy?

We must take our ears
seriously.

FAMILY   STORY

the beginning is true.

There was

a boy.

There was   a country

.

There was just a boy.
They took   words from   .

There was just a boy
and they took from   words

he could not speak with others
he could not know there were others
he was just a boy

a boy

alone.

                    that boy
            I   know
                 spoke

        take
our ears

M Y   STORY

Only   beginning is true.

           an island

   a boy.

          a train   a country

            a boy.
They took

                   his words
                        he could not speak   others
                        he could not know there
                        he was just a boy

alone.

I am   that boy

I   know

I   gave that boy

my (f)ears

OR

the beginning

an orphan
a boy.

others

know

he was just a boy

Tell me again Father
how we know these things.

I think I have a nervous heart,
a deerheart,
not   *a salmonheart,*
not   *a fish.*

When I was a girl
                    sometimes
I would die

And then
              when I was dead
I came back to life
I could not remember anything

I didn't know what kind of monster I was—
                                        I was some kind of monster
Were there woods?
              Were there seas?
                            Were there other bodies?

I imagine red trees
I am small under

              hunger grows

Were these my trees?
              My seas?
                            My other bodies?

I couldn't remember

I couldn't remember my other lifes
when I was only a girl

                    small and singular

AS FAR AS RECORDS GO

I.
The women in this story never had a chance, did they Michael?

It's sons we tell stories for.

>   Their skins and grasses and birch
>   bark rarely survive

>>   the archaeological record.

I found your sister in another record,
    in a family archive as it were
of dubious descent—

    82 iii. Nikifor (1897–1897)
    Occupation: Infant

    A grave shaped hole.
    Possibly, an empty house.
>>   (a painted box
>>   sealed tight against
>>   the weather:)

II.
Woman are always talking about the weather—

>   "Our people have made it through lots of storms and disasters
>   for thousands of years. All the troubles since the [*promyshlenniki*] . . .
>   like one long stretch of bad weather . . . like
>   everything . . . this storm will pass over some day."

>>   (On the island without trees, with wind no man
>>   could walk against, it rains two hundred and fifty days of the year.)

III.

Across the sea certain women were believed
    to have power over the weather:
        when weather was inclement, the women were exposed
    naked to the elements until weather changed—
or they died.

        (But I read this in some academic work or coffee table book
    on Aleut or Unangan art, so there might be a connection besides

Church records show—

IV.

Then there was Lillian Zellers—
    What kind of woman married an Indian
    in those days?

    (It was in the papers:) **INDIAN MARRIES WHITE GIRL**
            ALASKAN GRADUATE OF CARLISLE MAKES
            LEBANON YOUNG WOMAN HIS BRIDE.

I imagine someone in her family was tall—
    there's no accounting for our height if she were not tall.
        Or am I mistaking mothers again?

Even this is your story, Michael. There was no bearing daughters.

I suppose there must be somebody alive
    somebody would know—

    but letters are an accreted loss
        like skins and bark and mothers
    appeal to me as mystery.

V.
There was no bearing daughters. Turns out
    my black-haired grandma was no Indian
    after all. Not Aleut.

    I never met the men
    who gave me their bones.

VI.
My mother was a Mole.   (Names have been changed
                       but records are rare
                       -ly consistent—
                       enough blood to trace,
                       enough bodies in marked graves to remember,
                       enough,   enough.)

    And now I've gone and changed my name for legal reasons
    letting down my sons and daughters.
        (My husband would not have let them be salmon-fishers
        anyways.)

VII.
No, the women in this story never had a chance, Nikifor.
    It's fathers we make bodies for.

ARTICULATION OF DISTANCE
or, THE HERO IS DAILY CALLED TO MIND

These are the names that were written:

Mikhail

Vasiley

Vasiley

Tatiana

Iosif

Michael

Adrian

Nikifor

These are the names that survived.

These are the names that were spoken:

These are the names that were lost.

IN COMMUNION WITH THE NON-BREATHING

I went to the river   Michael   to see if you would speak to
me   but you weren't there   and the water   was to hide across
and I   wasn't big enough   to make a boat   to make my
body a boat   there was a boy and I couldn't fit him   in my body
          so I talked to no one   sent eyes air born to spy   but
there was no other   body   Tell me which shore did my father
call home   do my fathers   called home   dead   Slips
of the tongue   are telling are telling   And there's nothing for it but
the way I came   return me to the sea
                              infinity

I went to the river   Michael   you weren't there   so I wrote
this poem the way I thought you might speak the way   I thought you
might say   home   but you weren't there
and the water was high   I was alone   not at home

I don't know   Michael   what I'm doing   don't have
the words to say   is this where   I get in
My body   doesn't keep me warm   There
was Earth so   we must dig   Our hole   plan ts to
plant   weary future seeds   We must go
home   no body   us   here, and cold

It's lonely this way

I begin again

I give each fish a face

I give each a name

Even the dogs
know something isn't right
       when I spill the fish on shore

They push the puddles
with their mouths
       try to put the water back
in the shallow bodies

FAMILY GHOSTS

I was dreaming for a long time but now I can't remember.
I don't know

what words I had to say—

The water was my fault.
The earth was my fault.

And the Daughter, too,
           she was there
and me,

I was many in the dream

around a girl
           shaped
hole

in the cellar of an old rock
in the foundation.

In the Dream
often
      there is a fissure, a cave:

We were many in the earth
in the foundation

and I knew then,

blood in my mouth
           like dirt,
I was at fault

I buried the earth

I buried each
of my other selves

until the earth was full with daughters,
                granddaughters, great-
                        granddaughters—

Michael was my fault,
        was it my fault?

I buried each until I could not see or hear
and I emerged

singular   and silent.

After that there was no more
singing.

WAYS TO SUSTAIN

Break the body
along the ribs
                    offspine

Hang in the wind
until black
            to keep

Dry the skin
in borrowed sand

until water
tight

Smear the skin
with oil
            from the body

Carry   company –

            ivory eyed and
            whiskers and
                        treated blades
of grass
dipped in earth and billed at proper length

properly angled
properly
protected

in skin
boat

the sea
one

    you see –

Swallow the fish

feed whole
the hungry
mouths

belly full
with the sea –
there is only water
          salt
and air

Drag the bones ashore

———

The water was at fault
and the land was at fault

Only the current is fault
less

RE-ARTICULATION

With our homes we buried our children
with our hopes we buried them
that no one would find

Now there are no rooms for children
for burying

Michael go down the shore
you will find the fish
      the fish
that will make you home

                                     [Michael II who stayed in Alaska—
                                             occupation: fisherman
                                   —killed a shark on Wood Island
                                 and brought it to Miss Hannah.]

Michael go down the shore
Reach with your arms in the water until you feel the body

Slide your hands into its non-lungs
and pull its head from the water
                      pull

You are not the fish that swims in the maw

                                [Not many people consider the shark
                                         a fish.]

You are the maw
      the bridge many-teethed
and hungry

The way through the body
is through the body
      through blood
                 to the heart –

Michael of-the-water

MANIPULATING MANIFESTING
(RE)GENERATING LANDSCAPES

I.
I buried my bones.
        No trace was left.

I buried my bones and the landscape
        became settled in [its] disturbances.

There's no telling where the hand that digs might
        unearth the outline of a dwelling place,
                the shape of ivory in the process [of]

becoming human.
        It is not evident.

I buried my bones in the fault
        [where] they were of little consequence,
                more matters to settle

in the end.
        The land remembered only now.

I want to live somewhere old
        in the earth. On the water
                now there are many boats, [but] the vermin

they are hunting [is] dead
        with metal feet. His pelt
                [is] already sinking out of reach.

Old in the water. Let me sink
        [mine] in enough earth to bury [me].

II.

Mother, it was my fault. I buried each of my other selves
        until I couldn't see [ ] the earth was full.
        I was born(e) in this wound mother.

Singing made i[t] so. Steel singing. Destined
        men singing mercantile songs, manifesting
        swindling songs.

Singing say you see. Singing beautiful
        spacious skies, singing
        the brave in d(r)ead silence reposes.

You sang this land for me, (m)other. Each night
        I must find a new way to lay these arms
        stiff under the weight [of] my body.

III.

I don't know what I expected but at length I found myself a loan. I found
myself a part in a room of my own making, susceptible to drowning, to cave-ins.
I couldn't hold a shape my own among so many bones and matter besides.
The field turned relic into me.

IV.

           like this, Apaq?
can I wear these faces? which [way]
        shall I bend these bones?
does my skin show [through] these furs?
        do my metal feet b(ear) too much weight?
can I bend my arms in light of mo(u)rning?
           can I bend them in name for what I (k)now believe?

V.

Return every (last) bone to the l[and]
        I will shape my body in the sound [of]
           waves breaking the shore

[if] singing made it so
        these days will not be many
           no(w)

VI.
I wonder if you hear me, Apaq.
      I wonder if I say your [right] words.

Michael, will you row the boat (a)shore and dig a womb-shaped home
      with my arms
      for your arms
      for all the word worn arms

[until] the waters b(r)each our skin and sink these bones
      in their weight
      in the sand
      to begin again without blood in the print?

Only the beginning is true
each time

There was fire.

There was flood.

There was one
                she came from the water
                each time

She had to throw her own bones
over her shoulders

Each time we assume each rock
became human

Each time we assume
we resemble her

Each time the waters recede
we descend

Each time she waits to begin
                without fire   with our fire
                without bones   with our bones

                        without birthing monsters

ixtalix iganagii

ADDENDUM

HOW TO MAKE A MEMORIAL

These are the facts:

> On an island called either Awa'uq, or Refuge Rock, or
> [Your Massacre Site Here],
> Either six hundred died
> or two thousand.

(No one seems to agree, but the bones are still being dug up. No one lives on the island anymore. No one visits the island, except for *anthropologists*. It is littered with the bodies of the dead, this island that is "become numb.")

Afterwards, there was no question they were Russian.
Rather, there was no question they were made to be Russian.
That is to say, there was no question they were claimed under Russian
rule.

> (Though there were some who didn't know.)

(It's not that they are/were Russian but for a time it was easier to be
Russian. *Better be Russian.*)

The year was 1784. It couldn't even be called a war.

> It was a decisive military defeat.
> An isolated incident.
> Defensive tactics of a *merchant* ship.

> (Though some might say it was unusual for
> a Russian merchant ship to be so armed.)

It could be called a *decisive military victory*. In a history book, a *historian* calls it a decisive military victory. There were cannons and armed men and with their cannons and their arms and many deaths—exact numbers disputed— they obtained the hostages and the furs they came for, these *merchants*. They established business in "these hitherto unknown islands." (You could say that.)

They say Grigori Shelikhov was a man of *persuasion*.
It is said he was an effective *trader*.

(You could say it was "*unusual*.")

»

[from "A report to Emperor Alexander I from the Russian American Company
Council, concerning trade with California and the establishment of Fort Ross"
(translated)]

> "This settlement has been organized through the initiative of the Company.
> Its purpose is to establish a (Russian) settlement there or in some other
> place not occupied by Europeans, and to introduce agriculture there by
> planting hemp, flax and all manner of garden produce; they also wish to
> introduce livestock breeding in the outlying areas, both horses and cattle,
> hoping that the favorable climate, which is almost identical to the rest of
> California, *and the friendly reception on the part of the indigenous people,* will
> assist in its success."

The year was 1813. The climate was mild and invigorating. The way the wind
brushed the long grass and the waves broke on the shore (like *home*.)

It is said the reception was *friendly*.
They say it was a *success*.

»

Previously, let's say 1803, it was proposed that joint venture hunting expeditions
be undertaken along the Californian coast, using Russian supervisors and
Aleuty hunters. (One cannot point fingers and remain objective, such
documents and proposals always pleading the passive voice.)

The otter was found to be plentiful, which ensured it would remain the
Company's most profitable trade item,

> ("even if the quality of the fur was not as high as the Alaskan
> otter.")

The climate was mild and invigorating.

It is not said,
You could say it was just like home to the "Aleuty."
You could say it was home to the not Europeans who lived in those
and other places.

(They don't say that.)

»

Concerns regarding relations with the Indians proved *groundless* (in the passive
voice). The "Undersea People" treated the "People from the Top of the Land"
most *fairly*.

Reception was *friendly*. The indigenous people were most ready to *assist* in the
Company's *success*.

A deed was drawn and signed by the Russians.
This they say is *proof*.
It is said "the chiefs [were] very *satisfied* with the occupation of this place
by the Russians." [submitted as evidence: 1817 Fort Ross deed]

(What is not said, "this place" was Metini, ~~was~~ is the heart.)

Today historians *agree*, "the three-way culture of Native Californians, Native
Alaskans, and Russians at Fort Ross was chiefly one of genuine cooperation,
which some attribute to the religious values that had been instilled earlier in the
Russians and Aleuts, by clergymen in Alaskan Russian America."

1817. It was signed by the Russians, but the Kashaya *agreed*.
Only the Russians signed the deed, but rest assured Chu-gu-an, Amat-tan,
Gem-le-le *agreed*.

(Say *fairly*.)

»

Of course, Baranov, a man of enormous talent, courage, and stamina,
sent to Metini by Shelikhov,
who was both admired and feared by Russians, [and] Natives,
respectively,
was also a man of *persuasion*.

»

A hunting base was established on the rocky slopes of the Farallon Islands, some
30 miles west of the port settlement in the Saint's name—the patron of animals,
the environment, and stowaways—for a small host of Aleuts and Indians under
a foreman of the Company based in Fort Ross.

(terms to review: *armed men, hostages, furs, merchants*)

Members of the *artel* and their families were *rotated*, depending on the size
of the herds during hunting season. Depending on the *success* of the *hunters*.
It was a culture of genuine cooperation.
Chiefly.

(*indentured servitude, hostage exchange, cooperation, success*)

»

All in all, they say, everyday life was active and peaceful.
(If the hunting was *successful*.
If the indigenous peoples remained *friendly*.
If they were treated *fairly*.

If they were *cooperative*.)

»

1841. It is done.

The seals and sea otters were depleted by the Aleut hunters.
Farming was at best marginal.
And the United States objected (to the Russian presence).
[According to a newspaper in Oregon, Dec. 10, 1987.]

»

[Your Year of Genocide / Assimilation /Loss Here]. It is (not) done.
The [Aleuts] were depleted by [the seals and sea otters], by [government
legislation], by the hunters.
Capitalist gains were at best marginal.
And the United States objected (to indigenous presence).
[According to local sources, "It is said, they said."]

»

1976. The Heart is set aside as a historic site to be preserved for posterity.

"The mission of the Fort Ross Conservancy, Incorporated, is to promote for the
benefit of the public the interpretive and educational activities of the Russian
River Sector of California State Parks at Fort Ross State Historic Park and Salt
Point State Park.

Goals and Objectives:

1. Promoting public awareness and understanding of the natural and cultural
   [and colonial] history of Fort Ross State Historic Park and Salt Point State
   Park;
2. Supplementing, enhancing and conserving educational and interpretive
   [and memorial] activities relating to the Park;
3. Producing and making available to park visitors, friends, and interested
   people, by sale or free distribution, suitable [convenient] interpretive,
   educational and supportive [non-objectionable] materials and services,
   including, but not limited to, books, maps, pamphlets, visuals and
   recordings, consistent with the stated purposes of this Conservancy;
4. Supporting State Park Volunteers in Parks programs;
5. Supporting the development and maintenance of [re-]interpretive facilities,
   trails and library;
6. Preserving, conserving, enhancing, and restoring [all] the biodiversity and
   the natural [and indigenous] resources within the Park;

7. Sponsoring, supporting and assisting scientific research and investigations relating to Fort Ross and Salt Point State Park, [settler colonialism,] [indigenous displacement,] [allegations of mass genocide, also known as manifest destiny,] and the dissemination of this information to the public;

8. Raising funds to accomplish the Conservancy's mission and goals [to redress these historical omissions through poetry or any available means]."

WAYS TO SKIN A FISH
A Genealogical Survey

1971. The Alaska Native Claims Settlement Act was signed into law by President Richard M. Nixon, constituting at the time the largest land claims settlement in United States history. Support of the Act included oil companies interested in an expedient resolution—one that would allow them to begin construction of the Trans-Alaska Pipeline. [ENROLLMENT QUALIFICATIONS/PROCEDURES/INSUFFICIENT BLOOD RECORDS]

Did you know before then, we were Aleut, father?

1. Mikhail CHEBOTNOI. Mikhail died on 1 Jun 1856 r.o. in Unalaska Church District, Alaska. Occupation: walrus hunter and local baidarshchik; local starshina; early settler of Korovin Island.

   Mikhail married unknown (?).

5. Vasiley Mikhailovich CHABOTNOY. Born on 21 Jul 1830 r.o. Vasiley Mikhailovich died on 21 Jul 1877 r.o.; he was 47.

   On 10 May 1849 r.o. when Vasiley Mikhailovich was 18, he first married Fekla Soshin, daughter of Egor Sosnin and Matrona (?), in Unalaska Church District, Alaska. Born on 3 Jun 1830 r.o. in Atka Church District, Alaska. Fekla died in Unalaska Church District, Alaska on 10 Jul 1868 r.o.; she was 38.

22. Vasiley "2nd" CHABOTNOY. Born on 13 Jan 1863. Vasiley 2 died bef. 1901; he was 37.

   On 14 Apr 1882 r.o. when Vasiley 2 was 19, he married Akelina Lodochnikov, daughter of Abram Lodochnikov & Lukiia Mershenin, in Belkofski Parish, Alaska. Born on 1 Jun 1865 r.o. in Unalaska Parish, Alaska. Akelina died bef. 1901; she was 35.

1823. Russians originally settled Aleuts at Belkofski to harvest sea otters. When Vasiley 2 married Akelina, it had three stores stocked with San Francisco treats and a Russian Orthodox church.

1-5.i. Vasiley's occupation is unknown. His grandfather was a walrus hunter and local badarshchik; local starshina; early settler of Korovin Island, named by the Russians, died 1856 in Unalaska Church District. Age unknown. Date of birth unknown. First contact with Russians unknown. That Mikhail is the first record suggests he was the first to bear the Russian surname. *The first historical Chabitnoy. Mischievous non-salmon fisher. "Salmon fisher" has more elegance in its etymological repercussions than walrus hunter. Though walrus-hunter commands a different kind of awe.*

(-5.ii.) Vasiley's father's occupation is unknown.

5.iii. It is not unlikely that Vasiley 2 was, shall we say, recruited, to hunt otters near Belkofski. Or rather, to harvest them. *I wonder what would be the ring in Russian of "fur farmer"?*

I have it on good authority that Aleuts, or Unangans, whichever we were, never ate otters, that to do so would be considered cannibalism, otters believed to be human souls in a previous life.* An Aleut soul could be reincarnated five times (before they were saved by the Russian Orthodox priests, of course). I also have it on good authority—that is, from the Catholic education system—that Indians *were very resourceful, very responsible; when it came to harvesting their kills, they didn't waste a thing. (Though this might have been a covert lesson in clearing our plates—if we couldn't send our food to Africa, we could at least aspire to be noble—.) So who were the cannibals in the Russian Alaskan Theater? Who was eating the otter flesh?*

1.iv. Korovin Island has a land area of 26.197 sq mi and is uninhabited by humans.

What was Vasiley's grandfather doing on Korovin Island? Who was he working for and why? What were his motives? Was he a man who commanded respect?

1-80. v. The straight-line distance from Unalaska to Belkofski is approximately 192 miles. From Belkofski, it is 80 straight-line miles to Korovin Island, 423 straight miles to Kodiak.

1867. When the Russians relinquished sovereignty over Alaska, Alaska's fur wealth was still intact.

[1885. Alaska regions assigned to religious denominations by US gov.; opening way for Woody Island Baptist Mission, 1893.]

1911. Sea otters had all but disappeared.

80. Michael CHABITNOY. Born on 16 Sep 1885 r.o. in Unga, Aleutian Islands East Borough, Alaska. Michael died in Lebanon, Lebanon County, Pennsylvania in 1920; he was 34.

They built the mission, but had trouble finding children.

Occupation: Hershey Chocolate factory employee. Education: Carlisle Indian School.

How do we arrive at Michael, from Vasiley (the "2nd"), from Vasiley 1, from Mikhail?

Michael married Lillian ZELLERS. Born in 1892. Lillian died in 1978; she was 86.

They had the following children:

172 i. William C. (1912–1979)
173 ii. Gordon (1919–1983)

1-5??. vi. According to the Alutiiq Museum's language studies website, under *ghost* (or *tanraq*), "A person's soul is in their breath and can be reincarnated five times before reaching eternal rest in the sky world. According to traditional beliefs, a human soul that wants to be reborn pulls a boat up onto the shore."

Undoubtedly, Michael was spirited from the islands first by boat, before train. Was he aware of his actions? Did he speak Alutiiq? Is this the right word? Which words did he carry in his breath to Carlisle?

80. vii. If he were not a chocolate moulder, a foreman, a factory man, an orphan, Michael Chabitnoy, oldest and only surviving child of Vasiley 2 and Akelina, died of TB at age 34, might have been a hunter, a fisherman, a trapper, a child, a soldier, a drunk, unsettled. *Grandfather, Father, Son, Brother. Appealing outside mystery—*

173. Gordon CHABITNOY. Born on 25 Jun 1919. Gordon died in Lebanon, Lebanon County, Pennsylvania-? in Mar 1983; he was 63.

Gordon married Christine Krall.

They had one child:
365 i. Robert

[Record of Pennsylvania Aleuts ends. Sixth generation missing in surviving document. No way of assigning number to seventh generation without disturbing existing order.]

---

* *The same man, in his furs and and bentwood hunting hat with many seal whiskers protruding, told me on good authority, if we lose our language it is unclear if we can still be Unangak. I always thought we were Alutiiq anyways. Mother says these things skip a generation.*

NOTES

FOX HUNTING: This text, including footnotes, has been lifted out of the transcription of a story told by Stepan Prokopyev to Waldemar Jochelson on the island of Attu in August 1909, collected in *Aleut Tales and Narratives*, edited by Knut Bergsland and Moses L. Dirks and published by the Alaska Native Language Center.

FAMILY HISTORY: Much of the language in these poems comes directly from Michael Chabitnoy's Carlisle Indian School student records, available on the Carlisle Indian School Digital Resource Center, carlisleindian.dickinson.edu.

["IN APPEARANCE, CHABITNOY'S CLAIMS..."]: The language used in references to Michael Chabitnoy's physical appearance and the validity of his status are borrowed from various newspaper clippings and press releases preserved among personal items passed through the family.

[OBSERVE THE INDIAN AS SUBJECT]: Photographs were a powerful propaganda tool in promoting Pratt's assimilation policies and obtaining financial and legislative support for the Carlisle Indian Industrial School at the old Army barracks in Pennsylvania. Students were photographed when they arrived, often with additional props not always culturally accurate to highlight their lives as *other* before Carlisle, and again after they were *civilized*. Between 1879 and 1918, over ten thousand children were taken to Carlisle in a deliberate attempt to sever them from their culture and history. Some were as young as four. Their hair was cut, their possessions were confiscated, and they were beaten for speaking their own languages, among other *reasons*. (Hayes Peter Mauro, *The Art of Americanization at the Carlisle Indian School*, University of New Mexico Press, 2011.) Nearly five hundred children died in Carlisle. Today, relatives are still fighting to bring some of them home. (Jeff Gammage, "Those kids never got to go home," *PhillyNews.com*, 13 March 2016.) By 1901, the Sugpiaq (Alutiiq) and Unangan (Aleut) peoples of the Aleutian Islands had been living with the Russians—so to speak—for over a century. No dramatic *before* picture of Michael has been found.

ELOCUTION LESSONS: Information regarding leading causes of death was taken from the Centers for Disease Control and Prevention website, cdc.

gov. When too much emphasis is placed on numbers and reports taken out of context or without additional information, these statistics may be misleading. ~~A recent study conducted by Dr. James Cunningham of the University of Arizona Department of Family and Community Medicine and the University of Arizona Native American Research and Training Center has found that "Native Americans' binge drinking and heavy drinking habits are equitable to those of whites" and that "in fact, the rates of abstinence from drinking were higher in Native Americans than in whites," thus suggesting the higher rate of chronic liver disease among Native American populations may warrant further research into additional factors. Of course,~~ the obvious remains: people are people. ~~(Natalie Robbins, "UA study disproves old stereotype of increased alcohol use in Native American populations," *The Daily Wildcat*, 18 February 2016.)~~

[DID YOU MAKE YOURSELF WIND TO MAKE UP YOUR SIZE?]: The anecdote regarding Mike Chabitnoy, a relative of the same name, and the shark was related by Hannah Breece in her memoir *A Schoolteacher in Old Alaska* (Vintage, 1997).

SURVEY OF RESOURCE ARTICULATION: Entire courses could and should be taught about the Alaska Native Claims Settlement Act (ANCSA) signed into law by Richard Nixon in 1971, or U.S. Code Title 43, Chapter 33. An entire project could be written around it, though I'm not sure I'm the one to write it. But like so many Alaska Natives, this piece of legislation has had a profound impact on my identity. My great-grandfather's history, like so much Native American history, is one of holes and erasures, of distortions and pejorative reports written by "discoverers." In 1901, Michael Chabitnoy was sent to the Carlisle Indian School, a school whose sole purpose was to erase all trace of the children's heritage, of who they were. To "kill the Indian and save the Man." After his sons endured as "half-breeds" in predominantly white central Pennsylvania, growing up without their father (Michael would die of tuberculosis just after my grandfather was born), my father's generation was able to comfortably pass as white. The erasure was nearly complete.

Then in 1968, while state and indigenous land claims were still being disputed, oil was discovered in Prudhoe Bay. Having perhaps learned from the failure of the reservation system to protect indigenous land claims in the lower forty-eight, 200 village corporations and 12 regional corporations were created and granted land in fee simple title and cash. Only Alaska Natives born before 1972 were eligible to be shareholders. Those born after could be enrolled as descendants, but with few exceptions, the only way they could receive their own shares was through inheritance or gift. ANCSA has received mixed reviews. Some have said the corporations themselves, a foreign Western structure thrown on a population with limited formal education and even less familiarity with Western business models, were designed to fail, and some nearly did. Others have faired better, but not without their share of community friction.

For my family, it has provided the means to reconnect with our Alaska Native heritage. What began as a scholarship led to more significant and complicated questions of deserving and belonging. What did it mean to check a certain box on a demographic form? What did it mean to say Aleut? To say Aleut instead of Alutiiq, Sugpiaq, Unangan? When ANCSA passed, my father enrolled as a shareholder, turning to Michael's Carlisle School records to determine which regional corporation we belonged to. When my sister and I began applying to colleges, he made sure we were enrolled as descendants. I have a card, flimsy plastic laminate, that reassures me that "The owner of this card is an Alaskan Native according to the Alaska Native Claims Settlement Act, 1971." Or, it doesn't reassure me. It only muddies the waters. A cousin who also grew up in Pennsylvania, who is my same generation, says it doesn't mean anything. His identity is based on numbers. He hasn't bothered to enroll as a descendant with a corporation. There is no section 1630 in the Alaska Native Claims Settlement Act, but the ramifications of this law are still being unpacked and questioned. I am still learning what it means to be "of the water," to be deserving of my family name. I am still learning how to answer *kinkut ilaten?* Do you know your relatives?

HISTORY LESSON (Umnak, Unimak, Unalaska, Krenitzin islands): Text borrowed from *Alaska Geographic: The Aleutians,* Vol. 7, No. 3. (1980).

AS FAR AS RECORDS GO: The quote in part II is from Alutiiq elder Barbara Shangin, speaking in the 1970s, quoted in *Returns: Becoming Indigenous in the Twenty-First Century* by James Clifford (Harvard University Press, 2013). I have replaced "Russians" in the original quote with *promyshlenniki* to refer more specifically to the fur hunters and traders and craftsmen that were the backbone of the Russian-American Company.

HOW TO MAKE A MEMORIAL: From 1812 to 1841, the Russian American Company operated from the colony of Fort Ross, on what is today the Sonoma Coast. Nearly a hundred Aleuts were *persuaded* to settle at the far southern colony to *work* for the Russian fur traders. "The Aleuts, with their 'passion' for hunting sea otter, were paid according to the number of otters they caught." For more on the history and mission of the Fort Ross Conservancy, visit www.fortross.org/history.htm.

WAYS TO SKIN A FISH, 1867: Lydia Black, "The Nature of Evil," in Shepard Krech III, ed., *Indians, Animals, and the Fur Trade: A Critique of* Keepers of the Game (University of Georgia Press, 1981).

Translations for the Alutiiq text throughout the book can be found on the Alutiiq Museum's Word of the Week page. Visit www.alutiiqmuseum.org/learn/alutiiq-word-of-the-week.

ACKNOWLEDGMENTS

I would like to thank my family for all of their support and encouragement. I would like to especially thank my husband, Daniel, who followed me halfway across the country to pursue a childhood dream. Sincere thanks also to my parents, Robert and Valerie, for instilling an early love of reading and a lately realized appreciation of history.

Thank you also to the faculty, staff, and all my teachers and fellow writers at Colorado State University. Especial thanks to Dan Beachy-Quick for his kind and careful reading and unwavering belief in the work, and to Camille Dungy for pushing me to realize the full scope of the work. Thanks also to Thomas Swensen for the conversations and patient answers to my persistent questions.

Thank you to the Peripheral Poets for giving me the chance to bring these words home, or nearly so, and for the new words they've encouraged and inspired, especially Sherwin Bitsui and Joan Kane for the courage to continue.

Thank you to the Koniag Education Foundation, whose support and mission first sent me to my great-grandfather's records and to reconnect with my relatives.

And thank you to Michelle Gil-Montero, for convincing me I was writing poetry after all, and for first introducing me to the infinite possibilities of the genre.

I would also like to thank the editors of the following journals, in which several of these poems were first published:

Pleiades for SHEBUTNOY

Red Ink for AS FAR AS RECORDS GO, IN COMMUNION WITH THE NON-BREATHING, & ~~MANIPULATION MANIFESTING~~ (RE)GENERATING LANDSCAPES

Mud City for BEFORE THERE WAS A TRAIN, FOX HUNTING, RE-ARTICULATION, & SHE GETS HER POWER FROM THE WATER

Permafrost for QAWANGUQ WITH FOX

Tin House for QAWANGUQ WITH HOUSE & [SHE COUGHED AND THE
WOMEN CAME OUT]

Gulf Coast for FAMILY ~~GHOSTS~~ HISTORY, [BOY, BEAR, BIRD? SHARK?
FOX?], [OBSERVE THE INDIAN AS SUBJECT], [THE EARTH WAS
HOLLOW], & [IT WAS WINTER AND I WAS SWEATING]

ABOUT THE AUTHOR

ABIGAIL CHABITNOY holds a BA in Anthropology and English from Saint Vincent College in Latrobe, Pennsylvania, and an MFA in Creative Writing from Colorado State University in Fort Collins, Colorado. She was a Colorado State University Crow-Tremblay Fellow, a 2016 Peripheral Poets Fellow, and a recipient of the John Clark Pratt Citizenship Award from Colorado State University. Her poems have appeared in *Hayden's Ferry Review*, *Red Ink*, *Tin House*, *Gulf Coast*, *Boston Review*, and others. Of Germanic and Aleut descent, she is a Koniag descendant and member of Tangirnaq Native Village, and grew up in Pennsylvania.